COUNTRIES OF THE WORLD

Cambodia

Gareth Stevens Publishing
A WORLD ALMANAC EDUCATION GROUP COMPANY

959.6
DES

About the Author: Dayaneetha De Silva researched Southeast Asia at the Australian National University. She continues to research and write about art, history, and everyday life.

Written by
DAYANEETHA DE SILVA

Edited by
GERALDINE MESENAS

Designed by
JAILANI BASARI

Picture research by
SUSAN JANE MANUEL

First published in North America in 2000 by
Gareth Stevens Publishing
A World Almanac Education Group Company
330 West Olive Street, Suite 100
Milwaukee, Wisconsin 53212 USA

Please visit our web site at
www.garethstevens.com
For a free color catalog describing
Gareth Stevens' list of high-quality books
and multimedia programs, call
1-800-542-2595 (USA) or
1-800-461-9120 (CANADA).
Gareth Stevens Publishing's
Fax: (414) 332-3567.

© **TIMES MEDIA PRIVATE LIMITED 2000**
Originated and designed by
Times Editions
An imprint of Times Media Private Limited
A member of the Times Publishing Group
Times Centre, 1 New Industrial Road
Singapore 536196
http://www.timesone.com.sg/te

Library of Congress Cataloging-in-Publication Data
De Silva, Dayaneetha.
Cambodia / by Dayaneetha De Silva.
p. cm. -- (Countries of the world)
Includes bibliographical references and index.
Summary: Introduces the geography, history, economy, government, culture, food, and people of Cambodia.
ISBN 0-8368-2322-2 (lib. bdg.)
1. Cambodia--Juvenile literature. [1. Cambodia.] I. Title.
II. Countries of the world (Milwaukee, Wis.)
DS554.3.D39   2000
959.6--dc21   00-020632

Printed in Malaysia

2 3 4 5 6 7 8 9 07 06 05 04 03 02

PICTURE CREDITS
A.N.A. Press Agency: 33, 56
Archive Photos: 12, 17, 58, 59, 76, 77, 80, 82, 84
Bes Stock: 2, 20, 24, 42, 47 (bottom), 73, 91
Susanna Burton: Cover, 35, 72
Camera Press: 71
Focus Team: 29, 87
HBL Network: 1, 3 (bottom), 13, 14, 15 (both), 18, 23, 26, 30, 34, 37, 47 (top), 49, 50, 57 (both), 62, 63, 70, 78, 79
Dave G. Houser: 3 (top), 7, 31 (both), 55, 60, 66, 69 (bottom)
The Hutchison Library: 6, 19, 27, 53, 64
Supharidh Hy: 83
John R. Jones: 43
Earl and Nazima Kowall: 22 (bottom), 48, 61, 65, 89
Photobank Photolibrary: 3 (center), 9, 10, 25, 28, 32, 39, 44, 45, 46, 54, 67
David Simson: 8, 21, 22 (top), 36, 40
Still Pictures: 75
Topham Picturepoint: 41, 52, 68
Vision Photo Agency: 11, 81, 85
Nik Wheeler: 4, 5, 16, 38, 51, 69 (top), 74

Digital Scanning by Superskill Graphics Pte Ltd

Contents

AN OVERVIEW OF CAMBODIA

Cambodia is in the southwestern part of the Indochinese peninsula of Southeast Asia. Also known as Kampuchea, Cambodia is what remains of the Khmer Empire that ruled over large parts of Southeast Asia from the ninth century to the fifteenth century. The fabulous Khmer ruins of Angkor are masterpieces of world art and architecture. After almost three decades of war and destruction, Cambodians today are rebuilding their land, lives, and culture. Although poverty is still a problem in Cambodia, economic growth spells hope for the future.

Opposite: **Cyclos, or bicycle rickshaws, are an inexpensive form of transportation in Phnom Penh.**

Below: **Saffron-robed monks are a common sight in Cambodia.**

THE FLAG OF CAMBODIA

The two blue bands at the top and bottom of the Cambodian flag represent royalty, while the red band in the center represents the nation. White symbolizes Buddhism, Cambodia's main religion. The fourteenth-century temple complex, Angkor Wat, sits in the center of the flag. Angkor Wat is the most important symbol of Khmer culture and civilization. The building represents the structure of the universe according to the Hindu religion of the ancient Khmer kings. The current flag has been used since September 1993, following the first election in two decades.

Geography

Cambodia is located on the Southeast Asian mainland and covers 70,238 square miles (181,916 square kilometers). It is flanked by Thailand in the northwest, Laos in the north, and Vietnam in the east. The southwestern coast faces the Gulf of Thailand. The capital of Cambodia is Phnom Penh.

Mountains and Plains

Most of Cambodia consists of a basin-shaped lowland area, enclosed by mountain chains to the north, east, and west. The Cardamom range in the southwest contains Cambodia's highest peak, Phnom Aoral, which stands at 5,948 feet (1,813 meters). The Elephant Mountains are found in the region between the Tonle Sap and the Gulf of Thailand. The Dangrek range marks a natural border with Thailand. Dense tropical forests cover most of the mountains. Their rapid deforestation is of international concern.

The central plains are the most densely populated areas of Cambodia. The plains are a mixture of cultivated land, paddy fields, and grasslands dotted with sugar palm trees.

Below: **Paddy fields dot the plains near Kampong Chhnang in central Cambodia.**

The Mekong

The Mekong River and its major tributary in Cambodia, the Tonle Sap (Great Lake), bring life to the heart of Cambodia. The Mekong, which is approximately 2,700 miles (4,350 km) in length, is one of the mightiest rivers in the world. It begins in the Tibet Plateau in China and flows through Myanmar, Thailand, Laos, Cambodia, and Vietnam. It forms the Mekong Delta in Vietnam before flowing into the South China Sea.

In the heart of the central plains lies the Tonle Sap, the largest inland lake in Southeast Asia. The Tonle Sap acts as a natural flood reservoir for the Mekong. During the rainy reason from mid-May to early October, the Mekong overflows its banks. When this happens, the Mekong River reverses its direction of flow and fills the Tonle Sap via the Tonle Sab River. The Tonle Sap expands to double its size and floods the surrounding countryside. During the dry season, water in the Tonle Sap flows back into the Mekong, leaving behind fertile soil. This annual flooding of the Mekong leaves rich alluvial deposits in the central plains.

Above: The rich aquatic life in the Mekong River and the Tonle Sap sustains Cambodia's fishermen and their families.

THE FLOODING OF THE TONLE SAP

The reversal of water flow in the Mekong River has traditionally been an occasion for mass celebrations attended by the king. The annual Water Festival is a huge event in Cambodia, with dragon boat races and parades. The Tonle Sap itself is a central part of Khmer life and culture.
(A Closer Look, page 54)

Seasons

The climate of Cambodia is typically hot and humid year round. Monsoons bring dramatic changes in rainfall, creating two seasons: a wet season and a dry season. Between 75 and 80 percent of the total annual rainfall is brought by the southwest monsoon between May and October. The arrival of the northeast monsoon in November ushers in the harsh dry season. The average temperature is 80° Fahrenheit (26.7° Celsius), but it is cooler in the highlands. Temperatures can also drop a few degrees in the lowlands during the dry season.

Floods and Droughts

Cambodia sometimes suffers devastating floods or droughts when the monsoons are not regular. Rainfall is not evenly distributed across the country, and the mountainous areas, particularly the Cardamom Mountains, receive the most rain. Irrigation helps distribute and control water resources to various agricultural crops, and great potential still exists for increasing the range and amount of crops grown.

Below: **Floods are common during the rainy season.**

Left: The roots and branches of giant strangler figs and ceiba trees threaten to destroy ancient Khmer temples in Angkor.

DISAPPEARING FORESTS

The forests of Cambodia are being logged at an alarming rate and with careless disregard for its people and its ecosystem. Logging is often carried out illegally. The resulting deforestation threatens the habitats of many species and causes soil erosion.
(A Closer Look, page 52)

Plants and Animals

Cambodia's extensive forests contain abundant plant and animal species. Animals in Cambodian forests include tigers, clouded leopards, elephants, monkeys, civets, bears, and many varieties of reptiles and birds. The Tonle Sap and the Mekong River support a huge variety of freshwater fish, amphibians, and waterfowl. Many animal species are being threatened by increasing population pressure, deforestation, hunting, and land mines.

Cambodia's forests contain commercially usable timber, as well as trees that are prized for their aromatic oils and resins. Since 1970, increased deforestation has led to a considerable reduction in forest cover.

THE KOUPREY

The kouprey, a large wild ox, is an elusive animal living in the remote forests of Cambodia. It is regarded as an icon of the ancient Khmer civilization. The kouprey is an endangered species. Scientists have mounted dangerous and costly expeditions to hostile border areas to gather specimens, photographs, or information on the animal, with little success.

History

Early History: Funan and Chenla

Little is known of the early history of Cambodia, but it is believed to have been inhabited since about 4000 B.C. In the first century A.D., the Khmer, whose origins are still being debated, began to have contact with Chinese and Indian groups. Various elements of Indian culture were to have a lasting influence on the Khmer.

Funan was the first Cambodian empire and the first great empire in Southeast Asia. Funan was heavily influenced by Indian political ideas and ruled until the seventh century, when it was absorbed by the kingdom of Chenla, which covered what is now northern Cambodia and southern Laos. During this period, the Khmer lived in rival city-states ruled by kings and princes.

The Rise and Fall of Angkor

In 790, the Khmer ruler Jayavarman II came to power. His reign signaled the beginning of the golden age of the Khmers. His dynasty, based around the city of Angkor, lasted from the ninth century to the fifteenth century. The rulers of the Angkor kingdom saw themselves as *devarajas* (de-vah-rah-jahs), or god-kings.

Left: **In the twelfth century, Jayavarman VII renamed the Angkor kingdom's capital city Angkor Thom. Today, the ruins of the ancient Khmer temples of Angkor Thom draw hordes of tourists every year.**

Left: The French made Norodom Sihanouk king of Cambodia in 1941. King Norodom Sihanouk (*left*) is pictured here with French colonial secretary Coste-Flouret (*right*) during a visit to France in June 1948.

The kings of Angkor strove to outdo one another by expanding their territory and building splendid monuments and public works. One of the greatest monarchs was Suryavarman II, who built the temple complex of Angkor Wat. At its greatest extent, the Angkor empire controlled much of present-day mainland Southeast Asia.

After the death of its last great ruler, Jayavarman VII, Angkor began to fall apart. The final blow came in 1431, when Siam (Thailand) conquered the last capital, Angkor Thom. Cambodia's royal capitals were alternately subject to Siamese or Vietnamese invasion or interference for almost five centuries.

The French and World War II

In 1864, Norodom became king. In 1884, the French persuaded King Norodom to accept protectorate status for Cambodia, saving the country from being divided between its two neighbors. Cambodia became part of French Indochina, along with Laos and Vietnam, and gained stability. The French did little to develop Cambodia as part of its colony of Indochina; however, they did build roads and establish rubber plantations in the country.

Japanese forces briefly occupied Cambodia during World War II (1939–1945). After the war, the French reclaimed Indochina, and in 1945, France granted Cambodia autonomy.

ANGKOR WAT

The kings of Angkor left a great artistic legacy that has endured as the central symbol for Cambodians. Fine Khmer temples and ruins are found as far away as northern Thailand. The Siamese sacked Angkor Wat in 1430, and for centuries afterward, the ruins were almost hidden by dense jungle. Although Cambodians knew of the great city of Angkor, it was inaccessible to most until French archaeologists revived interest in the complex.

(*A Closer Look*, page 44)

Independence

Norodom Sihanouk was made king at the age of eighteen in 1941. He declared Cambodia's independence on November 9, 1953. In 1955, Sihanouk gave up his throne to form a political party. In elections held that same year, Sihanouk's party won every seat in the National Assembly, and he became prime minister.

Civil War in Cambodia and Vietnam

In 1970, General Lon Nol overthrew Sihanouk, sparking the five-year Cambodian civil war. Sihanouk created a government in exile in China and allied himself with Cambodian communist forces led by Saloth Sar, better known as Pol Pot.

In the early 1970s, the Vietnam civil war between South Vietnam and communist North Vietnam spilled into Cambodia when the United States, which supported South Vietnam, began a massive bombing campaign to destroy North Vietnamese border stations in Cambodia. The bombing campaign wrought vast destruction in Cambodia, and approximately half a million Cambodians were killed.

Below: **A national solidarity rally was held in the national stadium at Phnom Penh during the Cambodian civil war of the 1970s.**

Left: From 1975–1979, Khmer Rouge guerrilla forces persecuted and killed thousands of innocent Cambodians.

The United States' bombing campaign also resulted in increasing support for Pol Pot's forces. In 1975, Lon Nol's government collapsed, and the Communist Party of Kampuchea took control of Phnom Penh and the country. Sihanouk returned to become Cambodia's head of state but resigned one year later.

The Khmer Rouge

From 1975 to 1979, when the Khmer Rouge (kuh-MAIR rooj) controlled Cambodia, the country experienced the darkest years in its history. Led by Pol Pot as prime minister, the Khmer Rouge — the armed wing of the Communist Party of Kampuchea — turned Cambodia into a labor camp. Theirs was a regime of terror, genocide, and attempted cultural annihilation from which the country is still recovering. An estimated 1.5 million Cambodians died during the Khmer Rouge years, from execution, starvation, and overwork. The educated and professional classes were practically wiped out.

In 1978, Vietnam invaded Cambodia and pushed the Khmer Rouge toward the Thai border. The Khmer Rouge, however, continued to attack Cambodia and planted thousands of land mines that continue to kill and maim Cambodians today.

After 1979, Cambodians struggled to restore their country, but miserable conditions forced thousands to leave the country. Most ended up in refugee camps along the Thai border.

THE KILLING FIELDS

The Khmer Rouge and its deadly ideas began with a group of Khmer university students in Paris in the 1950s. Looking for radical solutions to poverty in Cambodia, these students adopted an extreme form of communism, in which all Cambodians were forced to work in the fields to achieve the Khmer Rouge's vision of agricultural self-sufficiency. The Khmer Rouge's rule from 1975 to 1979 was marked by extreme brutality and genocide.

(A Closer Look, page 60)

The First Elections

The Vietnamese withdrew from Cambodia in 1989, and a temporary coalition government — the Supreme National Council (SNC) — was formed, with Sihanouk as its president. In May 1993, the United Nations organized the first national elections in Cambodia in almost twenty years. A new coalition government was formed, with Sihanouk's son Prince Norodom Ranariddh as first prime minister and Hun Sen as second prime minister. Sihanouk was re-crowned in September 1993.

Cambodian Elections of 1998

The power sharing between Ranariddh and Hun Sen, however, was a tense one, and in July 1997, a two-day war broke out between soldiers from the two factions. Hun Sen ousted Ranariddh from office and took control. The international community was outraged, and the Association of Southeast Asian Nations (ASEAN) delayed Cambodia's entry into the association.

After a new election in 1998, Hun Sen became the sole premier of Cambodia, and Ranariddh was appointed the president of the National Assembly, part of the government's legislative branch. In 1999, Cambodia became a full member of ASEAN, a sign that it is beginning to stand as a united country. With the surrender of Khmer Rouge leaders in 1998, there is hope that the factions in Cambodia will finally work together to create a lasting peace.

LAND MINES

Today, Cambodia is beginning to put its chaotic past behind it, and the government is slowly rebuilding the country and its economy. Thirty years of war, however, has left a legacy in the millions of land mines that still lie buried. Every year, land mines maim or kill thousands of people, many of them children. Land mines also threaten the survival of the Cambodian people, because they render as much as one-third of the farm land unusable. Today, de-mining organizations, such as the Cambodian Mine Action Center (CMAC), have the massive task of ridding Cambodian land of hazardous land mines. (*A Closer Look, page 62*)

Left: Buddhist monks wait to cast their votes in the 1998 election.

Jayavarman VII (c. 1120/25–c. 1215/19)

Under the reign of Jayavarman VII, the Angkor empire was at its greatest extent. In 1177, Jayavarman VII defeated Cham forces in Angkor. In 1181, he was crowned king and set about rebuilding the capital. He adopted Mahayana Buddhism as his religion, but practiced religious tolerance. During his reign, extensive public projects were completed throughout the kingdom. Art and architecture also flourished during his reign, including the building of some of the most remarkable temples in Cambodia.

Pol Pot (1928–1998)

Born Saloth Sar to a peasant family in 1928, Pol Pot changed his name in 1963 when he became secretary general of the Communist Party of Kampuchea. Pol Pot became a communist in 1949 while studying in Paris. Between 1975 and 1979, he ruled as a dictator, overseeing the four darkest years in Cambodia's history. He wanted to restore Cambodia to its ancient glory but almost succeeded in wiping out its culture. Pol Pot remained the head of the Khmer Rouge while it was operating along the border areas. Few knew what Pol Pot looked like until 1997, when he was tried by the Khmer Rouge for ordering the murder of his colleague Son Sen and his family. The cause of Pol Pot's death in 1998 remains a mystery.

Pol Pot

King Norodom Sihanouk (1922–)

Crowned king in 1941 at the age of eighteen, King Norodom Sihanouk has played an important role in modern Cambodian history. In 1955, he abdicated his throne to lead Cambodia as its first prime minister. In 1970, his army chief of staff, Lon Nol, overthrew his government in a coup. During the Khmer Rouge years, Sihanouk was mostly under house arrest in Phnom Penh, and between 1979 and 1990, he was in exile in China. In 1991, when he returned to Cambodia after twelve years, Sihanouk was welcomed as the symbol of Cambodian unity. In 1993, he was re-crowned king, taking the throne he had given up forty years earlier.

King Norodom
Sihanouk

Government and the Economy

The System of Government

The Kingdom of Cambodia was established on September 24, 1993, with the assistance of the United Nations. The current constitution was adopted on September 21, 1993. The Cambodian government is a multiparty, liberal democracy under a constitutional monarch. The chief of state is King Norodom Sihanouk and the head of government is Prime Minister Hun Sen.

The king is ruler for life. His successor has to be of royal blood and is chosen by the Royal Council of the Throne. The Royal Council consists of the president and the first and second vice presidents of the National Assembly, the prime minister, and the chiefs of the Buddhist religious orders.

Below: **The magnificent Royal Palace in Phnom Penh has a large portrait of King Norodom Sihanouk on its facade.**

Left: **Cambodian Prime Minister Hun Sen reviews a guard of honor in 1997.**

The king appoints the prime minister and his Cabinet members. The Cambodian government is made up of twenty-five ministries and two state secretariats. The country is divided into twenty provincial units and three municipalities.

The Branches of Government

The government consists of legislative, executive, and judicial branches. The legislative branch is made up of the National Assembly, which has 122 members elected by popular vote for five-year terms, and the Senate, which has sixty members appointed through agreement by the key political parties. The National Assembly is chaired by Prince Norodom Ranariddh, while the Senate is chaired by Chea Sim.

Executive power is in the hands of the prime minister and his Cabinet, the Council of Ministers. The judicial branch is independent of the legislative and the executive branches of government. Key judicial decisions are made by the Supreme Council of the Magistracy, which was formed in 1997. It is chaired by the king.

POLITICAL PARTIES

The two main political parties in Cambodian are the Cambodian People's Party (CPP) led by Chea Sim and the National United Front for an Independent, Neutral, Peaceful, and Cooperative Cambodia (known by its French acronym FUNCINPEC) led by Prince Norodom Ranariddh. Other important political parties include the Sam Rainsy Party (formerly the Khmer Nation Party), the Buddhist Liberal Party, the Populist Party, and the Khmer Citizen Party.

Left: Rubber is one of Cambodia's main export products.

The Economy

Cambodia's economy is based on agriculture, chiefly rice growing. Cambodia's main exports are timber, garments, rubber, soybeans, and sesame. Rice, fruit, and vegetables are also sold across the borders to Vietnam and northeastern Thailand. Another growing source of income is tourism. Cambodia imports items such as construction materials, petroleum products, machinery, and motor vehicles. The country's main trading partners are Singapore, Japan, the United States, Thailand, Hong Kong, Indonesia, and Malaysia. Cambodia also continues to receive substantial economic aid from many countries.

Cambodians are among the poorest people in the world. In 1997, the estimated average per capita income was about $700. More than 80 percent of Cambodians are farmers, growing rice and other crops, such as sugarcane and bananas, for their own consumption. A small percentage work in small-scale industries such as rice milling, fishing, wood products, rubber, cement factories, gem mining, and textiles.

Economic Reforms

The government is now pursuing economic reform through a partnership with the private sector. It is trying to integrate the Cambodian economy into regional and world economies by

RICE GROWING

The agricultural sector employs more than 80 percent of Cambodians. Rice is the most important agricultural product. Rice cultivation was the foundation on which the ancient Khmer kings built the remarkable Khmer civilization, and it has been the center of Cambodian culture for centuries.

(*A Closer Look*, page 70)

WEAVERS OF ART

Traditional silk weaving is once again becoming an important part of the economy. In villages outside Phnom Penh, women between the ages of sixteen and forty are trained to dye silk and weave. After their training, they may either join a silk weaving business or receive credit and equipment to open their own businesses.

(*A Closer Look*, page 72)

investing in education, transportation, energy, and rural development. The Cambodian government is also trying to attract additional foreign aid and investment.

Although much has been achieved in the past few years, the challenge facing Cambodia's economy is huge. Everything needs to be repaired or improved, from cities, industries, and roads to schools and the political system. On the other hand, there is much potential wealth in its resources, such as hydropower, sustainable logging, and tourism. The country's biggest problems are extensive unrecorded logging activities and illegal gem sales.

CYCLOS, BOATS, AND OXCARTS

Years of war have destroyed or damaged the roads and railways in Cambodia. Cambodia's waterways are important means of transportation in the country. In Cambodia, it is still common to see heavily overloaded buses and trains or crops and people being transported in oxcarts. (*A Closer Look, page 50*).

Left: Fishing is an important source of income for Cambodians living along the Mekong River and the Tonle Sap.

People and Lifestyle

With about 11.6 million people, Cambodia has the second smallest population in Southeast Asia. The majority of Cambodians live in villages in the lowland areas around the Tonle Sap and the Mekong River. Most Cambodians are Khmer, while the rest are mainly Vietnamese, Cham, Chinese, or tribal Khmer.

Ethnic heritage is just one of many factors that determine a person's social position in Cambodian society; age, special gifts, education, and wealth are also important. Showing respect to

Below: Young Cambodians go to work. Khmer women wear a large scarf, called a *krama* (krah-mah), to protect their heads and necks from the sun.

one's elders or social superiors is part of daily life. Cambodia's small middle class includes business people and middle ranking government officials. Many Chinese, Vietnamese, and other minorities belong to the middle class. The small upper class group consists of aristocrats, high-ranking government officials, and military and religious leaders.

Ethnic Groups

About 90 percent of Cambodians are Khmer, making the population the most homogeneous in Southeast Asia. The ancestors of the Khmer are believed to have come to the

PHNOM PENH

For centuries, Phnom Penh had the most diverse and sophisticated population in Cambodia. The old ways of life ceased in 1975. Today, most of the people living in Phnom Penh come from villages, and business in the capital is booming again.

(A Closer Look, page 68)

Mekong Delta from what is now Thailand. The modern Khmer is a blend of many cultural and ethnic groups. Traditionally, most Khmer are farmers and live in the countryside. Today, many are moving to Phnom Penh and other cities.

The Chinese have been in Cambodia in large numbers for only two centuries, but they have been part of Cambodian history since the time of Angkor. Many Chinese married Khmer and adopted Khmer customs. Before 1975, they were the largest minority and controlled the economy. Many Chinese who escaped during the war years emigrated to other countries. Most Chinese live in Phnom Penh and other towns; many are traders and bankers.

Below: **Boys cool off in the shade of their home.**

Many Vietnamese settled in Cambodia during the Vietnamese occupation of Cambodia. Centuries of mistrust and often hostile relations, as well as the different beliefs and practices of the two cultures, still stand between the Khmer and Vietnamese. Many Vietnamese work in business and other skilled jobs, but those who live in the Tonle Sap area fish for a living.

The Cham are descendants of refugees from the Kingdom of Champa, which once ruled a large part of Vietnam. They have had friendly relations with the Khmer. The Cham are Muslim. Many Cham make their livings by farming, fishing, breeding cattle, or trading. Some specialize in metalworking or weaving.

It's a Child's Life

Cambodian families are close-knit. Cambodian children are given a lot of affection and freedom until about the age of three or four, when they are expected to bathe and feed themselves. At the age of five, they start looking after their younger siblings. By the time children are seven or eight, they have learned to be obedient and respectful toward their elders and monks. At the age of ten, girls are expected to help their mothers with simple household tasks, while boys have to look after the family's livestock.

Between the ages of eleven and nineteen, a boy may become a temple servant before going on to become a novice monk. Teenagers usually play with members of the same gender, except during festivals, when girls and boys take part in group games.

Above: **A young girl takes care of her baby brother.**

Respecting Traditions

Age is an important marker in Cambodian society. Old age brings high status. The young must show respect for their elders, even when the age difference is slight. An elderly couple may invite their youngest child's family to move in and run their household. In return, older Cambodians often help care for their grandchildren and devote more time to service at the temple.

Below: **A house in the Cambodian countryside sits on stilts.**

Above: **A bridal couple goes through the rituals of a traditional Cambodian wedding.**

Gender Roles

Although the husband is the head of a Khmer household, the wife has a lot of authority, especially in managing the family budget. Men and women have different, but not necessarily unequal, roles in Cambodia. Some tasks are performed by either men or women, but others are performed together, such as preparing rice fields for planting and buying and selling land.

Cambodian Weddings

Traditionally, parents and matchmakers chose young people's life mates. Today, young people in the cities often choose their own marriage partners. Traditional Cambodian weddings last three days. Modern wedding ceremonies are shorter.

Wedding ceremonies begin in the morning at the bride's home. Buddhist priests offer a short sermon and recite prayers of blessing. Ceremonial rituals include cutting hair, tying cotton threads soaked in holy water around the bridal couple's wrists, and passing a candle around a circle of married couples to bless the newlyweds. After the wedding, a banquet is held.

Education

Girls are still a minority in Cambodian schools. A Cambodian child begins school at the age of six or seven. Primary education lasts for six years, followed by six years of secondary education. All public education is free. A typical primary school serves two or three villages, and there are only about three high schools in each district.

The Cambodian education system is still recovering from the effects of the civil war and the Pol Pot era, when children had to labor in the fields and schools and libraries were destroyed. Few educated Cambodians survived and many emigrated. Before the

Below: **Students listen attentively in a village school. Today, more Cambodians girls are being educated.**

war, education was not universally provided, and boys learned to read and write Khmer at temple schools. Today, there is a shortage of teachers and schools, as well as a shortage of books and basic materials.

A typical Cambodian classroom is a bare room with rows of long wooden desks and benches. Children sit next to each other, and four or five children may have to share one textbook. Pens, pencils, paper, and other items are also scarce. A large number of students do not finish primary school. Many children drop out to help their parents earn a living. Even fewer of those who finish primary school go on to high school.

CHILDREN AT WORK

Cambodian children often have to drop out of school to work and support the family. Many work as street vendors, factory workers, and tour guides. International and local organizations are working to get children out of the work force and back to school.
(A Closer Look, page 48)

Higher Education

Recently, several higher education institutions have been established or restarted. High school graduates can study a wide range of courses. Some of the programs taught at these institutions are funded with foreign assistance. The Royal University of Phnom Penh was founded in 1960 and has eleven disciplines; six are in the field of social sciences, and five are in the field of natural sciences. Other institutes offer everything from business to technical courses and medicine. Not all courses are conducted at schools. Most adult Cambodians have had little education, and some courses are held at workplaces.

A Well-Rounded Education

The importance Cambodia is giving to learning can be seen in efforts to educate Cambodian children and adults throughout the country. Rescuing, reviving, and passing on traditional Khmer culture is also an important part of a Cambodian education. The revival of temple schools means that some children will again study the ancient Pali script and Buddhist scriptures. Children of craftspeople or artists learn skills directly from their parents, while others are selected to study at the School of Fine Arts. Outside school, Cambodian children are taught to be obedient and to play useful roles in their families.

Above: **Talented young people are selected to attend the School of Fine Arts in Phnom Penh. Here, they are trained as classical dancers, musicians, and artists, in addition to learning the basic school syllabus.**

Religion

The majority of Cambodians are Theravada Buddhists. Minority groups are free to practice their own religions. There are around 60,000 Roman Catholics in Cambodia and a smaller number of Protestants. The Cham are Muslim. Most Cambodian Chinese are Confucianists or Taoists. Along with their faiths, most Cambodians also believe in a supernatural world of spirits.

Buddhism

Buddhists see the universe and all life as part of a cycle of eternal change. They follow the teachings of Buddha, an Indian prince born in the sixth century B.C. Buddhists believe that a person is continually reborn, in human or nonhuman form, depending on his or her actions in a previous life. They are released from this cycle only when they reach nirvana, which may be attained by achieving good karma through earning merit and following the Buddhist path of correct living.

Earning merit is an important part of Buddhist life. Buddhists in Cambodia earn merit by giving money, goods, and labor to the temples, or by providing one of the two daily meals of the monks.

BUDDHISM IN CAMBODIA

During the Khmer Rouge years, many monks were executed and many temples were destroyed. Today, Buddhism is once again the dominant religion in Cambodia.
(A Closer Look, page 46)

Below: Buddhist monks are highly disciplined and must follow 227 rules in addition to the ten basic precepts of being a good Buddhist. Monks cannot take part in entertainment. They lead simple lives dedicated to Buddhism and the temple.

Children often look after the fruit trees and vegetable gardens inside their local *wat*, or temple. Boys can earn merit by becoming temple servants or novice monks for a short time. Most young men remain monks for less than a year.

Islam

The Cham converted to Islam around the fifteenth century due to Malay influence. Islam is a complete way of life that encompasses religion and culture. The Muslim God is Allah. The Cham are Sunni Muslims, one of the two main branches of Islam, and they can be divided into two groups. The traditionalists consider Allah to be all-powerful, but they recognize other non-Islamic gods and believe that magic and sorcery can be used to avoid or heal sickness and misfortune. The orthodox Cham follow a stricter Islamic way of life. They speak the Malay language, adopt Malay customs, and go on pilgrimages to Mecca, Islam's holy city in Saudi Arabia.

MAGIC, SPIRITS, AND FAITH HEALERS

Cambodians of all faiths tend to believe in the power of magic and the supernatural world. Small shrines holding offerings to appease the spirits are displayed throughout the country.
(A Closer Look, page 64)

Language and Literature

The majority of Cambodians speak Khmer, the official language. However, an estimated 35 percent of Cambodians over the age of fifteen cannot read or write Khmer. French was once the second language used by educated Cambodians, and it is still spoken by older Cambodians. English is replacing French as the second language, especially in Phnom Penh.

The Khmer Language

The Khmer language was first written during the period of Indian influence. Khmer is written in a script derived from a southern Indian alphabet. The earliest surviving example of the Khmer script is in a temple inscription made in A.D. 61. Khmer was influenced by the Indian classical languages, Pali and Sanskrit. Like all languages, Khmer has changed through Cambodian history, and today it contains Thai, Chinese, and French words.

Left: **A woman stops to examine a poster in Cambodia.**

Left: **A Cambodian man reads a Khmer newspaper outside a temple in Angkor.**

Khmer has no tones or tenses. It has twenty-three vowel sounds and thirty-three consonants, many of them in combinations that cannot be easily transcribed into English. The script is written from left to right, often with no separations between words. Many Khmer words change, chameleon-like, depending on their context, and there are as many as one hundred words for rice!

Khmer Literature

Much of traditional Khmer literature is based on the *Reamker*, an adaptation of the Indian Hindu epic, the *Ramayana*. The stories of the *Reamker* can be found throughout Cambodian art and culture.

Many Cambodians cannot read or write, so Khmer stories are related through folk tales. Many Cambodian folk tales have moral messages and are often retold through art forms, especially shadow theater. Proverbs are also very popular among the Khmer. These illustrate folk wisdom and the sayings of the Buddha.

The low literacy rate and the death or exodus of most of Cambodia's intelligentsia have stunted the development of modern Khmer literature. Since 1980, however, Cambodian authors have published several hundred literary works. Many of these works are written in English and French. Almost all recent Khmer novels and autobiographies are about family tragedy during the Khmer Rouge era, refugee camp life, or resettlement in a foreign country.

29

Arts

Art, religion, and life come together in Cambodia every day. Art is not just something that is placed in a gallery. It can be seen in the brilliant colors of handwoven silks, in the carvings that decorate wooden houses, and in the Cambodians' love of dance, drama, and music. Cambodian traditions of sculpture, mural painting, architecture, and weaving have been passed on from generation to generation. Much of Khmer art has a Buddhist or Hindu religious theme. The temple complex of Angkor Wat, with its exquisite architecture, statues, and carvings, is one of the world's leading artistic treasures.

Recovering the Past

During the Pol Pot years, much irreplaceable knowledge was lost. The Khmer Rouge executed famous artists, dancers, and master musicians, destroyed musical instruments, and burned down libraries. They also destroyed audio tapes, movies, and all other records of Cambodian music and culture because they were

Below: **A worker touches up the roof of the Royal Palace.**

30

reminders of previous regimes. In the past ten years, Khmers living in Cambodia and abroad, along with foreign individuals and institutions, have made efforts to record and recover Khmer music and other art forms.

Classical Cambodian Art

In traditional Cambodian art, the artist remains anonymous and the work usually has a religious or sacred meaning. For example, little is known of the sculptors and artists of Angkor. Statues of the Buddha or other figures are carved in traditional postures, each of which conveys a particular religious idea.

Some common motifs of classical Khmer art include *apsaras* (ap-sah-rahs), or heavenly dancers; *nagas* (nah-gahs), or mythical snakes; *garudas*, or animals that are half bird and half human; and *singhas* (sing-ngahs), or guardian lions. These motifs and others still appear on Khmer handicrafts today, including silver objects, textiles, wood and stone carvings, woven baskets, silk garments, and leather goods.

Below: Many relief sculptures in Angkor depict apsaras.

Traditional Crafts

In the old royal port of Kampong Hluong, silversmiths use imported silver to make intricate bowls in the shape of fruit, elephants, and other animals. They also make fine plates, trays, cutlery, and candlesticks.

West of Siemreab, women weave baskets from jungle vines. Girls and women cycle into the forests to cut and gather the vines, then they prepare and weave them. The girls sell the finished baskets outside their villages.

Cambodian wood carvings show their belief in the spirits of trees, flowers, and other inanimate objects. When a house is built, a miniature house is also made. This miniature house is where offerings of food, flowers, and incense are placed to keep the spirits happy.

Traditional Music

The Khmer love for music goes back to the kingdom of Angkor. The apsaras carved on the walls of Angkor hold musical instruments, similar to those that exist today.

Music plays an extremely important role in the religious beliefs of the Khmer. Musical arrangements are not written down, but passed on from musician to musician. Six types of ensembles

Above: **Skilled Cambodian crafts people make wonderful jewelry, baskets, and Khmer pots, such as these.**

HEAVENLY DANCERS

Cambodians believe they can speak to their gods through dance. The mythical seductresses of Angkor were dancers called apsaras. The apsaras are central figures in Cambodia art and are almost as famous a Khmer symbol as Angkor Wat. These women represented the Khmer ideal of feminine beauty. Apsaras are believed to live in heaven, where they entertain Khmer heroes and holy men.
(A Closer Look, page 56)

are popular in Cambodia, and certain ensembles are present at important occasions, including weddings, funerals, and spirit worship sessions. The famous *pin peat* (pin pe-aht) ensemble accompanies court and masked dances. The pin peat ensemble consists of quadruple reed oboes, a xylophone, gongs, a small barrel drum, a large barrel drum, and small cymbals.

Recently, there has been a revival of Khmer popular music. Khmer bands made up of young Cambodians experiment with new instruments and new sounds and show the influences of Western, Thai, and Chinese pop music.

The Sobbana Foundation

Members of Cambodia's royal family are important patrons of the arts. The Sobbana Foundation, headed by Princess Norodom Mari Ranariddh, is a shelter for war orphans. The foundation operates three training centers in Phnom Penh. The foundation has trained more than four thousand women in weaving and sewing, and it has revived the Khmer arts of basket making, wood carving, woodworking, and stone sculpting.

Piseth Pelika was one of the most famous and talented Cambodian artists. Pelika was a singer, dancer, and actress. She was murdered in July 1999, and her funeral was attended by royalty and common people alike. Her death is seen as a tragedy for Cambodian culture.

Below: This painting depicts a scene from the *Reamker.* On the left is Hanuman, the monkey god, and on the right is a queen mermaid with three retainer mermaids.

Leisure and Festivals

A Simple Life

Most Cambodians do not or cannot afford to go on vacations. Their cycles of work and rest are seasonal and depend on the tasks to be done at home and in the fields. Most Cambodians have only known peace for a short time, but they are a fun-loving people and use any opportunity to gather, chat, play with their children, cook, and have special meals together. They also save money to celebrate their festivals with gusto.

Childhood Fun

Girls and boys in Cambodia play games that children everywhere do, such as jumping rope or participating in running contests. Although some city children may enjoy video games and other toys, most Cambodian children play with whatever they can find around them, using their imaginations to the fullest. Children in fishing villages enjoy playing and swimming in the rivers and lakes near their homes.

Below: **Many Cambodians living in the cities enjoy going to movie theaters on the weekends.**

Moving Pictures

Televisions are becoming common in urban households, but relatively few people in rural areas have them. Families and neighbors usually gather around one television set to watch local and regional soap operas and other programs.

Cambodians also love to watch movies. In the 1960s, Sihanouk himself produced and starred in many films.

Shadow Puppet Theater

Almost a combination of a movie and a play, the shadow puppet theater tells the stories of the *Reamker*. Although popular with Cambodians, shadow puppet theater was prohibited during the Khmer Rouge era and is rarely seen today. In the past, a single performance often attracted hundreds of thousands of spectators and lasted several nights. At these performances, children and adults mingle and chat with friends and relatives.

The art of shadow puppet making is passed down from generation to generation. Common characters include gods, demons, spirits, and other mythological figures. In one performance of the *Reamker,* up to one hundred and fifty puppets are used! The narrator is accompanied by an orchestra and is the real star of the show. He — the narrator is always a man — acts out all the parts and sings all the songs. Great narrators are revered. No women are allowed to take part in the performances.

Sports

Cambodians enjoy all kinds of games and sports, but venues and facilities for sports are mostly informal. For example, a volleyball game can take place with only two people, a ball, and a string tied between two trees in an open space.

After decades of war, organized sports are experiencing a revival. Many organized sports activities are still confined to Phnom Penh and the larger towns. The Olympic Stadium in Phnom Penh is the main center for organized spectator sports, such as soccer and basketball. Occasionally, teams of wheelchair-bound basketball players and other athletes who have lost limbs during the war compete. Most Cambodians cannot afford to participate in organized sports because they have to work to support the family, but they enjoy watching the matches.

Soccer

Soccer, known as football in Cambodia, is a popular sport. A semi-professional team plays between January and June. The Cambodian Football Federation was founded in 1953, but its activities were hampered by the years of political upheaval. The national team has been making a comeback in recent years and has participated in international matches, such as the Southeast Asian Games and the World Cup Qualifiers. In 1998, Cambodia played against China and Lebanon in the Asian Games in Thailand. The Cambodian national team has not won many games in recent years, but Cambodians take pride in their team and watch many games.

Above: **Universities and schools organize football league games between November and April.**

Motorcross

Motorcross or motorbike racing has gained a wide following in the past two years, with regular competitions held in Phnom Penh's Olympic Stadium. Motorcross races are also held in provincial centers. There are several training grounds where young racers hone their skills, watched by family, friends, and sports fans.

Dragon Boat Racing

The most colorful sporting event is the annual dragon boat race during the Water Festival. Teams of rowers compete in long dragon boats. Male and female teams compete to the cheers of spectators along the riverbank. The rowers, clad in their team uniforms, row rhythmically with long paddles.

Below: **Dragon boats line up for the start of the race.**

Kickboxing and Other Sports

Kickboxing is popular in Cambodia. Most Cambodians believe the sport originated in their country. In kickboxing, the boxer uses his feet, rather than just his fists, to attack and defend.

Other sports played throughout the country include badminton, which is often played along roads or in any vacant space; cycling; shooting; and tennis. Some forms of Chinese or Japanese martial arts, such as tae kwon do, are also practiced.

Along with the increasing popularity of the southwestern beaches, sea sports are on the rise. Scuba diving sites are being developed around Sihanoukville.

Left: **Monks bless the boat crews during the Water Festival.**

Major Holidays and Festivals

Cambodians look forward to their holidays and festivals. The first festival of the year is the Chinese and Vietnamese New Year. It is celebrated in January or February. Many shops are closed, and processions are held in the towns. National Day is celebrated on January 7 to commemorate the fall of the Khmer Rouge and the anniversary of the last sermon of Buddha.

The two largest festivals are held in April: the Khmer New Year and Pisakh Bochea. Although the Khmer New Year is a religious festival, it is also a time for having fun, and everyone dresses up in their newest or best clothes. Pisakh Bochea is the most important Buddhist festival. It celebrates the Buddha's birth, his enlightenment, and his attainment of eternal bliss.

KHMER NEW YEAR

Buddhist rituals and visits to the local temple play a major role in many Cambodian festivals. The biggest celebration in the Cambodian calendar is the Khmer New Year. (*A Closer Look, page 58*)

People gather at temples to participate in religious processions, receive blessings, and make offerings of flowers and food.

Another main festival is the beginning of Buddhist Lent, or Chol Vassa, in July, coinciding with the beginning of the rainy season. Many young men begin their period of monkhood on this day. The end of Buddhist Lent is in September and is celebrated with boat races in some places.

There are other, smaller festivals celebrated by non-Buddhist Cambodians. One of these is the celebration of the birthday of the founder of Islam in Odongk. The Cham of Odongk decorate trees with ornaments to represent their ancestral beliefs. The Muslim Cham also celebrate other Islamic festivals, such as the end of the fasting month and the birthday of the Prophet Muhammad.

For three days, starting on October 31, Cambodians celebrate King Sihanouk's birthday. Public offices and museums are closed on the first day of the celebrations. Independence Day falls on November 9. This national holiday commemorates Cambodian independence from French rule. On this day, floats and parades make their way through the streets of Phnom Penh.

Left: **In Cambodia, elaborate ceremonies and processions are held to celebrate the inauguration of temples, such as Wat Ku Tlok near Angkor.**

Food

Since the kingdom of Angkor, Khmer cuisine has been based on the sophisticated cultivation of rice. Thai, coastal Malay, and southern Vietnamese flavors are all present in Cambodian cuisine, but the most important influence on Cambodian cuisine has been Chinese food. The French colonial presence has left a taste for French food in the towns, with French food such as baguettes, pâtés, and café au lait readily available.

In the towns, snacking at all hours of the day and night is possible because of the large number of hawkers. In Phnom Penh, all types of cuisine are available in a range of restaurants, with French and Chinese food the favorite choices.

A Typical Cambodian Meal

Well-off rural Khmer have several meals a day. The first meal consists of a piece of fruit or cake. The first full meal is eaten at about nine or ten in the morning. Farmers eat a large meal at noon and have supper with their families on returning home at around 5:00 p.m. Poor rural Khmer have only two meals a day.

Each meal consists of rice, accompanied by soup. Rice may be less thoroughly milled than it is in many other rice-eating

MARKETS AND STALLS IN CAMBODIA

A wide variety of food is sold in markets and stalls across Cambodia. The largest market building in the country is the Central Market in Phnom Penh. Besides food, many different kinds of goods are sold there, including antiques, jewelry, and clothing.
(A Closer Look, page 66)

Left: Rice dumplings in all shapes and sizes are available in Cambodia.

40

Above: **These boys enjoy a midday meal.**

countries, and consequently, contains more vitamins and roughage. The most common accompaniments with rice are vegetables, fish, and fish-based products, such as *tuk trey* (tak trey), or fish sauce; *prahok* (prah-hok), or fish paste; and shrimp paste. Meat and poultry are considered more expensive luxuries, and they are used sparingly or for special occasions. Hot peppers, lemongrass, mint, and ginger add flavor to many Khmer dishes, and sugar is added to many foods. Several kinds of noodles are also eaten. The basic diet is supplemented by vegetables and fruit, which grow abundantly throughout the country. Sweets and desserts are usually made from palm sugar and coconut milk, and are prepared on special occasions.

There are no courses at a Cambodian meal. All the dishes are laid out together with the rice, and people help themselves to the dishes, adding a little bit of everything to their bowls of rice. The majority of people still eat what they grow, raise, or catch. Cambodians get together for communal feasts during festive occasions.

A CLOSER LOOK AT CAMBODIA

Cambodia is now at peace, but the shadows of war are long. The horrors of the Khmer Rouge years are being exorcised slowly. Life in Cambodia is changing gradually. Children are going to school again, and families are living together in peace. The arts and crafts of Cambodia have also been revived.

The coming of peace, the reinstatement of the king, and the grandeur that is Angkor have had an impact on people's lives and hopes. Increased numbers of tourists are coming to see Angkor Wat, and elegant hotels are being built. Cambodia needs the money from tourism, but it is not clear how tourism will change the daily lives of the people.

With Pol Pot's death in 1998 and the impending trial of surviving Khmer Rouge leaders, Cambodians may finally be able to put the destruction of the past thirty years behind them. Poverty still plagues the country, however, and buried land mines threaten the lives of Cambodians daily.

Opposite: **Boys may serve as novice monks at a very young age.**

Left: **These young Cambodian boys have fun during break time in school. Many children, however, are required to work to supplement the family income.**

Angkor Wat

Angkor Wat was one of the greatest monuments built by the Khmer kings, who at one time controlled much of mainland Southeast Asia. It was designed by King Suryavarman II's architect, financed by war, and built from a wax model by artisans, workers, and slaves, who transported huge stones in three thousand oxcarts. The entire complex took thirty-seven years to build.

The Stories of the Stones

The stones of Angkor Wat tell endless tales. They speak of richness and war, of kings and their laboring people, and of artists and dancers. The measurements and placement of the buildings at Angkor Wat — the moat, the length of the stone wall, the height of the towers — are precise and have magical and cosmic meaning to the Khmer. The original towers were probably covered in gilt and topped with banners and other decorations of religious

Below: **Constructed under Suryavarman II, Angkor Wat is the finest example of Khmer architecture.**

44

significance. The stones themselves were richly carved and colored. Inside the walls of Angkor was a whole city, the heart of which was the palace. The king rarely left the palace and was believed to have magical powers that protected him and his kingdom.

The "Discovery" of Angkor

Four hundred years after Angkor was invaded and sacked by the Siamese, Angkor Wat and other Khmer sites were almost hidden by the jungle. Some temples were used for worship over the centuries, but most were left to the invasion of jungle creepers.

In an age of exploration, Western interest was fired by descriptions of a magnificent ruined city deep in the jungles of Cambodia. In the 1860s, French naturalist Henri Mouhot stumbled upon the ruins of Angkor and brought back to France delicate watercolor paintings of the romantic city. Until the 1970s, French archaeologists and experts were mainly responsible for rescuing Angkor from the jungle.

Many of the treasures of Angkor were removed for safekeeping. Some are displayed at the National Museum of Arts in Phnom Penh. Beautiful statues, pieces of reliefs, carvings, and statues of the Buddha have made their way to museums in France and collections around the world. A great deal of ancient Khmer art, however, has been smuggled out of the country and sold to private collectors.

CONSERVING ANGKOR WAT

The temples of Angkor are fragile and need protection from the jungle, art thieves, and the harsh effects of the weather. They also need continual expert restoration.

The sand foundations of the temples have subsided, and water has seeped in. The soft sandstone itself has become crumbly with age. Bat droppings corrode the inner walls, lichen attacks the stone structure, and the roots and branches of giant strangler figs and ceiba trees entwine around, in, and through cracks, eventually pulling apart whole walls.

Angkor Wat is listed by the United Nations Educational, Scientific, and Cultural Organization (UNESCO) as a World Heritage site.

Buddhism in Cambodia

The Khmer have been Buddhist since the time of Angkor. Buddhist monks have often been involved in politics. In 1942, two monks were arrested for preaching anti-French sermons. The arrests sparked the first demonstrations of Cambodian nationalism. The Buddhist Institute and its newspaper also played an important role in Cambodian nationalism.

In 1975, there were 3,000 monasteries and 64,000 monks. Between 1975 and 1979, the Khmer Rouge banned all religion in Cambodia. Most monks were executed during the Khmer Rouge years, and many temples were destroyed or used for other purposes, such as storing grain.

Left: **In the early 1990s, Buddhist monks participated in peace marches to end war in Cambodia.**

WAT OUNALOM

Wat Ounalom in Phnom Penh is the most important temple in Cambodia. Wat Ounalom was built in 1443 to create a sacred place for a hair of the Buddha. Before 1975, five hundred monks lived there, but the Khmer Rouge attacked the temple and killed the patriarch. Most of Wat Ounalom has been restored, and it is still the headquarters of Cambodian Buddhism.

The temple was the seat of learning in Khmer culture and was the only place that the written Buddhist teachings were taught. Monks were often the only literate people in a village. Until the 1970s, monks taught Cambodians to read and write.

Unlike those who become novice monks for a short period, learned monks have a long history in Khmer culture. They are often skilled not only in the Buddhist scriptures but also in such arts as astrology and healing. By their way of living, monks demonstrate the ideal Buddhist way of life. Monks are usually present at all important ceremonies.

Buddhist Celebrations

Most Khmer celebrations are connected to important dates on the Buddhist calendar. Pisakh Bochea, held in April, is the anniversary of the birth, death, and enlightenment of the Buddha. Chol Vassa, another major festival, takes place in July; this is when the penitential season begins for monks, who remain inside temple compounds until September. The end of the penitential season is celebrated with offerings to monks.

Temple processions are colorful and often feature large puppet figures and bright costumes. Now that peace has come to Cambodia, people have been repairing the wats and giving them fresh coats of paint. Shops everywhere sell pink Buddha statues, incense, joss sticks, and other items used for prayer.

Children at Work

With a per capita income of $700 a year, Cambodia is one of the poorest countries in the world. All over Cambodia, boys and girls younger than ten years of age work alongside adults as farmers, fishermen, street vendors, porters, factory workers, plantation workers, and housemaids. Children cost less to hire than adults, and many have to work to provide for their families.

School versus Work

Child labor is a growing problem in Cambodia, where many children cannot afford to stay in school. Books and school supplies are too expensive for many families. School buildings are often in poor condition and are too far away for children who live in isolated villages. As a result, many people decide they cannot send their children to school. Instead, children are sent to work to provide food for the family.

Left: **In Cambodia, less than one-third of all students who enroll in primary school finish grade five. Many drop out of school to work as farmers, factory workers, maids, and street vendors, such as this young girl in Phnom Penh.**

The Working Child

Children work full days in brick and cement factories, in rubber plantations, at construction sites, and as stone cutters. At one fish-processing plant, children work from 7:00 a.m. to 5:30 p.m. Some children work part-time selling food, newspapers, and other market items. Many others have jobs in small restaurants, where they are paid low wages and work long hours. Young girls often work as maids in households. Young boys are found in all sorts of occupations, such as driving commercial boats on the Tonle Sap.

Growing numbers of children work in dangerous conditions and do heavy work meant for adults. Some of these children work alongside their parents. Not all occupations are harmful, however. For example, some children who work as tour guides at Siemreab use the money they make to help pay their school fees.

Local and international organizations have started programs to help Cambodia's working children, especially those who are orphans or homeless. These organizations are also trying to influence the Cambodian government to enact more laws to protect children.

Cyclos, Boats, and Oxcarts

Much of the road network in Cambodia was severely damaged during the war. Outside towns, boats are used during the wet season, while oxcarts are used during the dry season. Harvested crops are piled onto oxcarts and transported to mills. Ferries, buses, and trains are often packed with people and goods.

Trains are often overflowing with people on the roofs and hanging out the doors. Until recently, they were a frequent target of Khmer Rouge guerrillas and bandits. The two main railroad lines from Phnom Penh, which extend to Paoy Pet at the Thai border and to the port of Kampong Saom, are in need of repair.

City Travel

City streets are riddled with holes and craters and in need of repair or reconstruction. In Phnom Penh, many cars have

Below: **Trains are often packed with people and goods.**

appeared since the country's first democratic election in 1993. Most of these new cars belong to foreigners and to wealthy upper class business people in the cities.

Above: **In the cities, even trucks are used to transport people.**

The favorite mode of travel in the cities is by motorcycle, or by hiring a cyclo or moto. *Cyclo* is the French word for a bicycle rickshaw. The cyclo rider pedals his bicycle, pulling along his customer. Cyclos are cheap, and passengers can bargain with the rider for a satisfactory price. A faster way of moving around is by moto, or motorbike taxi.

Water Travel

Where roads are damaged, the most important form of transportation in the country is still by river. Boats, ferries, and ships ply the waters of the Mekong and the Tonle Sap. Passengers travel in small boats. Large vessels transport commercial goods, such as timber, agricultural produce, foodstuffs, and household goods, to and from Phnom Penh. The most important domestic ports are at Phnom Penh and Kampong Cham.

Disappearing Forests

In 1992, the World Earth Summit in Rio de Janeiro, Brazil, described Cambodia as the green lung of Southeast Asia. In 1965, over 75 percent of the country was covered with forest. Now, only 40 percent of Cambodia is forest land. If the current rate of deforestation continues, many fear almost all of Cambodia's forests could disappear early in the twenty-first century.

How has this come about, and what does it mean for Cambodia and its people? Much of the deforestation is due to unrestrained and, often, illegal logging. The forests of Cambodia are also disappearing because of development and settlement. Land is cleared for agriculture and for the construction of houses. Firewood is a source of fuel for many Cambodian homes because most do not have electricity. The chief culprit, however, is large-scale logging.

The Business of Wood

Neighboring countries, such as Thailand and Vietnam, need a great deal of wood for many industries, especially construction and furniture. With the political instability in Cambodia for the

Below: **Dense jungle surrounds the ancient temple complex of Angkor Wat.**

past ten or more years, it has been relatively easy to obtain forest logs cheaply and ship them out for a good profit. Some Khmer Rouge leaders, government officials, and logging companies from other countries have combined to chop down and remove valuable trees with great speed for generous profits.

All the partners in this business make a great deal of money, but almost none of it goes into the Cambodian economy. The rapid loss of Cambodia's forest cover is its most serious ecological issue. A change in weather patterns has occurred as a result of deforestation, and the delicate ecosystem of the Mekong and the unique fisheries of the Tonle Sap have been greatly affected.

Deforestation has caused the loss of valuable topsoil, as well as an increase in the number of landslides, which have destroyed houses and killed many people. Furthermore, the soil that is washed off is silting up rivers, making them shallower and contributing to heavier flooding. As the Tonle Sap's mangroves silt up, the lake's fish species are gradually losing their only spawning grounds. Deforestation is also stripping away the habitat of numerous species of flowers, plants, and animals. The disappearing forests also affect the tribal people who worship the spirits of the forests.

Above: **Workers unload wood at a railway station in Phnom Penh. Firewood is still the main source of fuel in Cambodian homes.**

THE SUN BEAR

The sun bear is one of the many animals whose habitat is threatened because of deforestation. Sun bears, named for the yellow crescents on their chests, are also in danger because they are sold for Chinese medicine in illegal markets. The government began a protection program in 1995 to prevent the sun bear from becoming extinct. In 1999, the first sun bear born in captivity showed that breeding could save the species.

The Flooding of the Tonle Sap

The Tonle Sap, the largest lake in Southeast Asia, lies at the heart of Cambodia. Over the centuries, much of Khmer history has revolved around the Tonle Sap. For six months of the year, the lake increases in size until it occupies nearly 3.7 million acres (1.5 million hectares) of Cambodia's land area.

The Retreat of the Waters

In spring, the monsoon rains swell the Mekong River so much that water flows uphill into a tributary and into the Tonle Sap. From June until the end of the wet season in October, the lake expands and becomes an inland sea. When this happens, the surrounding forests are partly submerged and hundreds of

Below: **The Tonle Sap is perhaps the largest inland fishery in the world. Large-scale commercial fishing takes place between February and May. Fishermen and their families live in floating villages near the shores.**

species of fish spawn and breed amid the underwater roots and trunks. This unique ecosystem also supports a large number of bird species that feed on the fish.

A large proportion of Cambodia's population earns a living from the lake through farming and fishing. The seasonal flooding brings with it many species of freshwater fish. When the water retreats, it leaves a rich alluvial residue around the shores, enabling rice cultivation.

Environmental Issues

The Tonle Sap has become a contentious topic. Some environmentalists, as well as the king, are asking for the Tonle Sap to be declared a World Heritage area. One proposal is that some parts of the Tonle Sap be declared reserves. The aims are to preserve endangered animal species, protect vital fish breeding areas, and prevent over-exploitation of the fisheries. Threatened species include several bird species, the clouded leopard, civets, the Siamese crocodile, and spotted cats.

Above: **Fisherfolk use a variety of nets, baskets, cages, and traps to catch fish. Fish are eaten fresh, dried, smoked, salted, or fermented into a paste.**

THE WATER FESTIVAL

The Water Festival dates back to the twelfth century, when King Jayavarman VII and his navy defeated waterborne invaders. This festival is celebrated with dragon boat races in Phnom Penh. At the end of the celebration, the king commands the waters to retreat.

Heavenly Dancers

Apart from Angkor Wat, the most famous symbols of Cambodia are apsaras, or heavenly dancers. Hundreds of these dancers are carved on the temple walls at Angkor. Their real-life counterparts in Angkor were so famous that the conquering Siamese took the dancers back to Siam as part of their war booty. It was thought that their dancing was so perfect that gods and humans were in harmony during a performance.

The Revival of Dance

The revival of Cambodian dance is a heroic tale. Cambodian dancers almost vanished during the Pol Pot era; many dancers and musicians were killed because they were connected to the royal court. Surviving members of the Royal Ballet taught dance to Cambodian children living in horrendous conditions in refugee camps in Thailand. In 1981, the National Dance School reopened to train a new generation of recruits, many of them orphans.

Below: Dancers perform at the Royal Palace.

56

Left: Traditionally, dancers were trained within the palace walls and danced only for the king. Today, the National Dance troupe performs at the National Museum of Art and, occasionally, at other public places.

Below: A dancer readies herself for a royal performance.

Dancers are trained from the age of six for a repertoire that includes romances and epics such as the *Reamker*. Children of all classes are accepted into the Royal Ballet dance troupe. They are taught special exercises to loosen their joints. They must learn the movements while their limbs are still supple. Cambodian ballet dancers can bend their fingers back to their wrists!

Dancers are usually women, but there are now some male dancers and characters. The dancers perform barefooted, and the movements of hands and feet are significant. Dance costumes are richly embroidered; expert dancers wear sumptuous silk and velvet costumes that have to be sewn on before every performance. For some roles, glittering headdresses and masks complete the ensemble.

Khmer New Year

In Preparation for the New Year

The Khmer New Year is one of the main celebrations in Cambodia. The Cambodian year begins in mid-April and is based on the lunar calendar — that is, it is linked to the cycles of the moon, not the sun. April also signals the end of the harvest, when most Cambodians, who are farmers, can relax and enjoy themselves. The exact starting date of the New Year is set by an astrologer. During the New Year celebrations, the people thank the departing demi-god or angel and welcome the incoming one. A small altar is set up in front of each house. Horoscopes and predictions are also made for the coming year.

Families begin preparing for the New Year weeks before the festival. Houses are cleaned and scrubbed thoroughly to remove bad or unclean spirits still lingering inside the household and causing mischief. Lengths of silk or other fabric are bought to make new clothes.

The Three Days of New Year

New Year celebrations last for three days. The first day, called Maha Sangkran, is the entry into the new year and is signaled

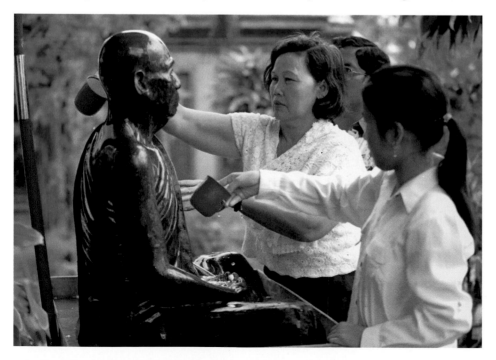

Left: **Buddhist devotees pour water over the statue of a revered Buddhist monk during the New Year celebrations.**

by the ringing of the bell or the rhythmic beating of the drum at the Buddhist temple. The bell ringing is a signal for the new angel to arrive. Plates of food are taken to the temple for the monks, and most people attend a New Year service, where they chant Buddhist prayers with the monks. Special dishes, such as peanut curry, are served on the first day.

Games are played throughout the first day, creating a merry atmosphere. One activity that children particularly enjoy is throwing buckets of water over each other and everyone else! Passersby are drenched in honor of the new year.

The next day, Vana Bot, takes on a more serious tone. This second day of the New Year is a time for more praying, for showing respect for one's elders, and for being charitable to the less fortunate. Children give parents, grandparents, and teachers gifts. People offer charity and forgive others for misdeeds.

The New Year festivities end on the night of the third day, called Loeung Sak. Buddhist monks bless small sand hillocks that people have built around the temple grounds. People wash statues of the Buddha with perfumed water to bring good luck, long life, and happiness. The washing of the statues also symbolizes the hope for sufficient rainfall during the next rice harvest.

The Killing Fields

The Khmer Rouge era, also known as the Pol Pot era, was the darkest period of modern Cambodian history. Cambodia cannot be understood without knowing about the "experiments" the Khmer Rouge performed on their own people. Today, Cambodians remember the hunger and fear. They mourn the loss of mothers, fathers, sisters, and brothers, as well as the disappearance of teachers, artists, musicians, doctors, and dancers. Their temples and mosques were destroyed, and their ancient manuscripts and libraries burned. An estimated 1.5 million Cambodians were killed or died from hunger or overwork during Pol Pot's rule. In the killing fields, or mass graves where victims were tortured and killed, the skulls and bones of these victims remain.

Left: **Exposed graves at the killing fields of Choeung Ek, near Phnom Penh, where tens of thousands of Cambodians were executed and buried.**

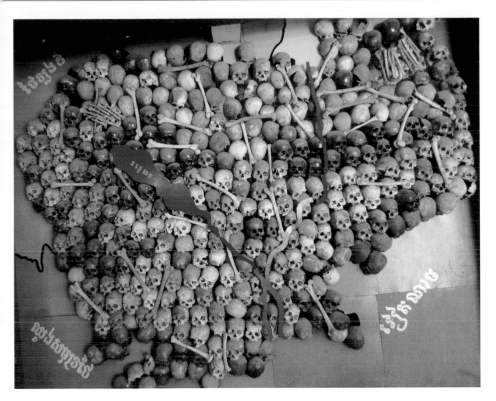

The Dark Years, 1975–1979

When the Khmer Rouge defeated the Lon Nol government and marched into Phnom Penh on April 17, 1975, many welcomed the end of the five-year civil war. The leader of the Khmer Rouge, Pol Pot, wanted to wipe out all traces of the old Cambodia and start a new society. Khmer Rouge soldiers forced everyone in the cities to leave their homes and walk into the countryside.

People were divided into camps and had to work as farmers and laborers in return for food. Life was strictly ordered and "social equality" was enforced. The people were ruled by the central Khmer Rouge organization, the Angka, and had to obey every order. If they did not obey, they were cruelly punished or killed.

The Annihilation of Culture

Many of those who were killed were educated people, such as teachers and monks, and people who had authority in the old regime. Educated or talented people had to disguise their identities and abilities to survive. One such person was Dith Pran, a journalist. His story of hardship and survival was made into an award-winning film, *The Killing Fields.*

TUOL SLENG

Tuol Sleng was a school that was taken over by the Angka and turned into a center for torture and interrogation. All of the prisoners taken there were accused of some "crime" against the Angka, to which they had to write a confession. Almost everyone who was taken there was executed even after confessing to crimes they did not commit. Most of those who were brought to Tuol Sleng were themselves Khmer Rouge, including leaders whom Pol Pot wanted to eliminate.

61

Land Mines

One of the most long-lasting and horrific effects of Cambodia's long period of war is that Cambodia is now one of the most heavily mined countries in the world. Land mines were planted by all factions in Cambodia's civil and guerrilla wars. Cambodian armies obtained mines and weapons from other countries. The land mines are concentrated in the northwest, especially in the Batdambang province, one of the most important agricultural areas before the war. An estimated 1,390 square miles (3,600

Below: **De-mining workers uncover their hazardous finds.**

square km) of land in Cambodia is mined. Most of the mines were deliberately planted to make the land impossible for use by each side's opposition.

A Land of Victims

Hidden in the fields, land mines explode when someone steps on them or when a field is plowed. The mines are designed to maim their victims, but when small children step on them or play with them unknowingly, the mines are powerful enough to kill. Many victims have had limbs amputated. In 1999, almost three hundred mine injuries occurred every month. Today, there are more than forty thousand amputees in the country.

The Cambodian Mine Action Center

Various overseas charities have been set up to help Cambodian craftspeople make inexpensive artificial limbs, which are normally made from wood. Mine clearing has been going on since 1990, but it is a costly and slow process. Experts estimate that it will take one hundred years to clear Cambodian land of all the mines. Experts are trying new methods, including the use of dogs to sniff out explosives. In dangerous areas, warning posters are put up,

Below: **A young boy learns to cope with the loss of his limbs.**

but mines are often planted in unexpected areas. In 1995, the first Mine Awareness Day was held to educate the people about mines.

The Cambodian Mine Action Center is the only Cambodian institution looking at the entire problem. It is responsible for mine marking, mine clearance, mine information, and mine clearance training. The United Nations has provided funds to help Cambodia eliminate its estimated 4–6 million mines and other unexploded devices. Its goal is to reduce the number of mine-related injuries and return the land to the farmers to live on and cultivate crops.

Magic, Spirits, and Faith Healers

Cambodians of all faiths tend to believe in an invisible world of ghosts, spirits, and magic. Cambodian Buddhist and Muslim beliefs are closely interwoven with these older practices. When Cambodians are ill or facing crises, they seek the help of the spirit world. The spirits are appeased by items, such as fruit and food, placed in shrines, but often Cambodians enlist the help of a medium or faith healer. It might appear that the Cambodian villagers' belief in this rich world of spirits is the real religion of the Khmer, but Buddhism, Islam, and other religions play important roles in the lives of the Khmer as well.

The Spirit World

Cambodians believe in several types of spirits, which show themselves through strange noises or happenings. There are ghosts, nasty demons, evil spirits (usually female), animal guardians, and *neak ta* (ne-ak tah), or ancestral spirits. Ancestral spirits live in the forests, hills, or trees. Each village has its resident spirit, and villagers often leave offerings of fruit and food in front of a roughly hewn stone taken from the spirit's dwelling place.

Left: **An *achar* (ah-char) displays a ritual model boat that is to be used in a ceremony.**

Left: **Some Cambodians have religious symbols tattooed on their bodies to ward off evil spirits.**

Good spirits must be shown respect, or they may cause mischief. If a child does not provide food for the spirit of his or her dead mother, for example, the spirit may cause misfortune to the child.

Of Achars and Krus

Various kinds of people help mediate between the real world and the spirit world: a *kru*, or spirit healer; an achar, or ritualist; a *thmup* (tee-moop), or witch; and a *rup areak* (rup ah-re-ak), or medium, usually male. A kru is often a former Buddhist monk with considerable prestige and power. He or she is a kind of alternative medical practitioner, curing illnesses with charms, amulets, and magic potions.

The achar is a master of ceremonies who attends births, weddings, and funerals. The rup areak is a medium possessed by supernatural beings with whom he communicates. Mediums are often important in the psychological and spiritual healing of Cambodians whose family members have died unnatural deaths. Through these rituals, they can "talk" to their family members.

Fortune tellers and astrologers are also very important. Many Cambodians consult them before making major decisions, such as marrying or building a new house. Many Cambodians believe in the power of magic amulets and charms. Khmer soldiers often wear amulets to ward off bullets when they are in battle.

Markets and Stalls in Cambodia

Everything under the Sun

Almost anything can be bought or sold at a Cambodian market. In every town, farmers, artisans, wholesalers, fisherfolk, and others gather at markets to sell everything from food to electronic goods to rare gems. Most Cambodians cannot afford to operate permanent shops. Many are farmers who need to be

Above: **A mobile stall delivers woven products right to street corners.**

in their fields for most of the year. People rent small spaces in markets or spread their goods on a cloth. Many transform their oxcarts into mobile stores. These mobile stores travel from place to place, stopping wherever there are interested buyers.

Something for Everyone

Most market stalls are run by women. Cambodian markets are busy, noisy, and colorful places. The larger markets in Phnom Penh and other towns, such as Batdambang and Siemreab, are livelier versions of modern shopping complexes. Smaller markets may sell only food or specialize in one product. For example, the Olympic market in Phnom Penh sells a lot of electronic goods and bicycle parts. Some markets are mainly for wholesalers — that is, they sell large quantities to shopkeepers or distributors who have stalls or shops elsewhere. Every market has food stalls.

The Central Market

Perhaps the most famous market building is Phnom Penh's Central Market. Also called the New Market, the Central Market was built by the French in 1937. From the outside, this huge market, painted in dark yellow, looks something like a Babylonian ziggurat. Inside, it is divided into sections

filled with shops selling all kinds of goods: checkered cloth scarfs; household goods; antiques; flowers; gold and silver jewelry; and food. Other popular markets in Phnom Penh include the Olympic Market and the Russian Market.

Some markets sell decorative, luxury, or souvenir items for local buyers and tourists. Items such as real or fake antiques, miniature reproductions of Angkor Wat, Buddhas, and silk cloth are often sold by craftspeople.

Markets are not just places to buy produce and other goods; they are also places where women and men meet to catch up on the latest news.

Above: **The huge Central Market in Phnom Penh has stalls selling all kinds of products, from food and flowers to electronic equipment and antiques.**

Phnom Penh

Phnom Penh has had a colorful history dating back to the mid-fifteenth century. In 1434, the Khmer nobility started a new capital in Phnom Penh, but it never achieved the grandeur of Angkor. However, its location at the meeting point of the Mekong and the Tonle Sab allowed it to become a center for trade. The port received goods, mostly from China, which were shipped in through the Mekong Delta.

The Sights of Phnom Penh

The principal sights in Phnom Penh are the Royal Palace, the Silver Pagoda, Wat Ounalom, the National Museum of Arts, and Wat Phnom. The Royal Palace was built by the French in 1884.

The Silver Pagoda was originally built by King Norodom to enshrine royal ashes. It was rebuilt by Sihanouk in 1962 to replace the old building. The floor of the pagoda is made up of 5,000 silver blocks. In the center of the pagoda is an emerald statue of

Opposite: **Located where the Tonle Sab and Mekong rivers meet, Phnom Penh is a major commercial center in Cambodia.**

Below: **Cyclo riders take a break in the bustling city of Phnom Penh.**

Buddha and a golden Buddha studded with 9,584 diamonds. King Norodom, acting in the fashion of a typical god-king of Angkor, had the Buddha cast with his own height and measurements.

Below: **The Independence Monument in Phnom Penh commemorates the country's independence from France in 1953.**

Modern Phnom Penh

In the 1960s, Phnom Penh was a beautiful city, with its broad boulevards, its riverside setting, and its mixture of elegant French colonial architecture and Khmer temples. During the Vietnam War, refugees swelled the population in Phnom Penh to almost 2 million. Between 1975 and 1979, the Khmer Rouge turned Phnom Penh into a ghost town. Many people were killed, while others were forced out of the city. Today, most of the people living in the city moved there from the countryside.

Most of the French colonial buildings and old houses in Phnom Penh are crumbling. Public health facilities are in poor condition and many other facilities and buildings need repair, but the city and port are bustling again. With the revival of the Cambodian economy, Phnom Penh now has the possibility of regaining its former prosperity and charm.

Rice Growing

The bowls of rice that Cambodian peasant families eat at every meal are the products of months of hard work and patience. Most family members participate in some way in the processes of sowing, harvesting, or storing the rice. The rice grains are usually not fully polished and thus have a pinkish or off-white hue. Families often sell the best rice, while keeping the broken grains for themselves.

The growing of rice has been a central part of Cambodian culture and life for centuries. The ability to cultivate crops of rice in the flood plains of the Mekong and its tributaries helped bring about the great Khmer civilization.

Left: **Rice planting is a backbreaking process.**

From the Seedling to the Grain

Rice is a difficult crop to grow because there are several stages, from planting the seedling to harvesting the rice. Each stage is a delicate and careful process. Rice seed is selected from the previous harvest or bought from a dealer. It is then soaked overnight before being sown into a carefully prepared nursery bed.

The nursery bed is often the richest land on the farm. After a month, the seedlings are carefully uprooted and transplanted in paddy fields. Before the seedlings are transplanted, oxen, cows, buffalo, or tractors plow and turn the soil. The fields are muddy, and each plant is manually pushed into the soil in neat rows. The work requires a farmer to stand bent over for long periods of time; this is probably the hardest part of the rice growing cycle.

Rice plants need a constant supply of water throughout the growing phase. The water supply is controlled by dikes and irrigation systems. Farmers have to watch the maturing crop carefully and guard it against pests, insects, birds, and other enemies. A farmer may move his entire family into the fields so that they can all keep an eye on the crop.

Rice harvesting is also hard work. Traditionally, farmers in a village would get together to harvest their crops. After harvesting, the stalks of rice are threshed to separate the grains from the stalks. Then the rice is brought back to the village to be stored in a barn. Once the harvest is in, the festivals begin!

Above: **Agriculture, particularly rice growing, is one of the most important uses of land in Cambodia.**

Weavers of Art

Cloth woven in Cambodia ranges from everyday cotton to unique works of art used in ceremonies. The head scarf, or krama, is the most common cotton garment worn by Cambodians. Cotton *sarongs* (sah-rohngs), or wrap-around skirts, are worn daily. Silk *sampots* (sahm-pots), loose-fitting garments wrapped around the waist, are worn by women on special occasions. Shimmering silk has always been a feature of Cambodian dress. Traditionally, brides would weave silk garments for their grooms; the bride herself would change her silk outfits many times during the three-day wedding. *Charabap* (cha-rah-bap), the most luxurious silk, is actually a tapestry woven with silver and gold thread for important ceremonies, such as those held at the royal court.

Opposite: **A shop in a local market sells cloth for common, everyday garments, as well as beautiful silk for more formal wear.**

Silk Weaving

Silk is woven in many areas of Cambodia, and each province is known for its particular designs, colors, and techniques. In times

Below: **A weaving school in Cambodia instructs students on the fine art of weaving.**

past, weaving villages could be identified by the mulberry bushes surrounding them. Silk is spun from the cocoons of silkworms that eat mulberry leaves. Color-fast dyes and silks are now imported from Vietnam and China, but efforts are underway to revive the traditional processes that produced fine, textured cloth of rich hues. The lengths of silk sold in markets in Phnom Penh are mostly from the Takev and Kampong Cham provinces.

Entire families work together to weave silk. In the home of a silk weaver, daughters begin learning the simple tasks when they are seven or eight. First, they learn to dye the silk threads and help to weave simple sampots. To become master weavers, students attend a school at Phnom Penh, where they learn to mix natural dyes and create complex patterns. Stripes, elephants, fish eyes, and jasmine flowers are some common motifs.

The most exquisite silks are made by famous weavers, who produce these cloths when they are specially ordered, often as prestigious gifts. These elaborate works of art use only the finest threads and natural dyes and can take months to complete.

SILK CUSTOMS

The wearing of silk follows age-old customs: bright purples, yellows, and reds are for younger women, and deeper colors are for older ones. In the past, sumptuary laws restricted particular types of clothing, fabric, or patterns for the exclusive use of royalty. This meant that only those of royal blood could wear the finest woven silks. Today, officials attending ceremonies at the Royal Palace still follow the traditional practice of wearing different colors on different days.

RELATIONS WITH NORTH AMERICA

The Vietnam War that raged during the 1960s and the early 1970s drew the United States into Cambodian territory. The United States' bombing of Cambodia in the early 1970s was the lowest point in relations between the two countries. After the Khmer Rouge years, both the United States and Canada took in large numbers of Cambodians fleeing their war-torn country.

In the last decade of the twentieth century, diplomatic and economic ties between North America and Cambodia improved. Both the United States and Canada provide aid and experts for various projects in Cambodia. Hundreds of thousands of Cambodians now call North America home — indeed, many of those born in North America see themselves as American or Canadian rather than Cambodian. Peace has also helped increase cultural exchanges between Cambodia and North America. The difficult years in relations between Cambodia and the United States have come to an end, and individual North Americans, as well as Cambodians, are working to help put an end to the years of war, poverty, and hunger in Cambodia.

Opposite: **The United States has provided large amounts of aid to Cambodia for the restoration of temple ruins in Angkor.**

Left: **Cambodians enjoy beverages from the United States and other countries. In this picture, a Cambodian man quenches his thirst with Micco Cola, the Chinese version of the American drink Coca Cola.**

The United States and Cambodia

No direct trade or other historical links existed between the people of Cambodia and North America until the twentieth century. The United States recognized the Kingdom of Cambodia in 1950. Between 1955 and 1963, the United States provided a large amount of economic and military aid to Cambodia.

During the 1960s, the United States helped South Vietnam fight against communist North Vietnam. Sihanouk did not want Cambodia drawn into this war and attempted to keep Cambodia neutral by refusing U.S. aid. Rather than provoke the North Vietnamese, he allowed them to use areas near the Cambodia-Vietnam border.

In 1970, Sihanouk was deposed and anti-communist Lon Nol took over Cambodia. The United States supported Lon Nol's government with massive military and economic aid (about U.S. $1.8 billion between 1970 and 1975). The Vietnamese saw U.S. support as a threat and proceeded to build up resistance forces on the border. These forces formed the Khmer Rouge.

The rural people, who revered Sihanouk as a hereditary ruler, did not receive much benefit from the American dollars that went into Lon Nol's military buildup. Their impressions of the United

Below: **U.S. troops patrol the streets of Snuol after its destruction by U.S. bombers.**

States came from the United States' massive, secret bombing campaign on the borders of Cambodia in the 1970s. About five hundred thousand civilians and soldiers were killed by bombs, and the rural people, terrorized by the bombings, became easy targets for recruitment by the radical Khmer Rouge.

In the 1980s, after the Pol Pot era and the Vietnamese invasion, tens of thousands of refugees, escaping from their destroyed country, were accepted into the United States.

Canada's Relations with Cambodia

Canada's relations with Cambodia date back to the time of Cambodia's independence in 1953. Until 1969, Canada was a member of the International Commission for Supervision and Control that oversaw the withdrawal of Vietnamese and French forces from Cambodia. Canada also helped to negotiate the Paris Peace Agreement of 1991, while some 300 Canadians assisted in the 1993 United Nations sponsored election in Cambodia.

Diplomatic Relations

In 1991, the United States opened its diplomatic mission in Phnom Penh. In 1993, the United States and the Kingdom of Cambodia established full diplomatic relations. The Canadians opened their embassy in Phnom Penh in 1994.

In the late 1990s, diplomatic relations focused on building democratic institutions, encouraging economic development, and helping Cambodia bring the surviving Khmer Rouge leaders to trial for crimes against humanity.

Aid to Cambodia

Both the United States and Canada provide generous amounts of aid and assistance to Cambodia to build up its economy and to help its people. USAID (United States Agency for International Development), Canadian volunteers, and other non-governmental organizations run many programs in Cambodia. In 1999, USAID spent about $12 million on aid and development programs to Cambodia. Many of USAID's programs help war and mine victims, especially amputees, war orphans, and widowed mothers.

Above: **The United Nations continues to have a presence in Cambodia, where peace is still uncertain. Here, children visit a U.N. guard at his post.**

Canadian Aid

Canada contributed some $9 million in development assistance to Cambodia from 1996 to 1997 and over $9 million in 1998 and 1999. Most of the money is used for food and de-mining programs.

The biggest Canadian project is run by a group of Canadian non-governmental organizations. The project is aimed at helping the people of Pouthisat province improve their lives through better medical facilities and other facilities.

Canada is also one of five countries active in the Cambodian Mine Action Center (CMAC). About 4 to 6 million deadly mines are believed to have been planted throughout the Cambodian countryside. The United Nations-sponsored CMAC trains Cambodians to de-mine their country and works with Cambodians to remove or defuse the bombs. Canada believes that helping Cambodians de-mine their country is an important step toward building a peaceful country. The Canadian team provides world-leading anti-mine technology, advisors, and engineers. It also sponsors mine awareness programs that teach people about the dangers of hidden land mines and how to move safely and carefully through the countryside.

Below: **CMAC volunteers help Cambodian amputees get used to their new artificial limbs.**

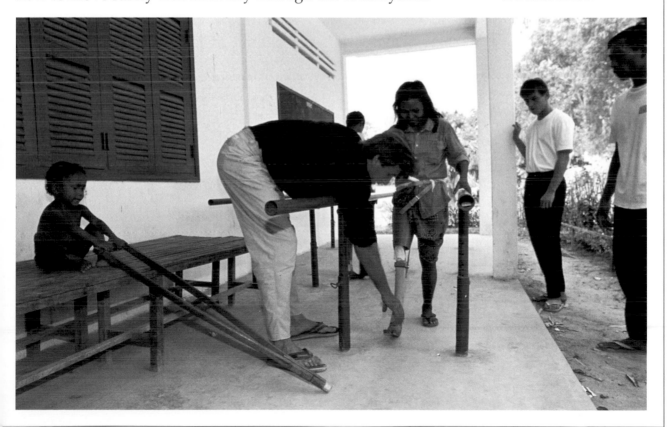

The Khmer Rouge War Crimes Trials

The United States government has been working to bring the remaining leaders of the Khmer Rouge to trial as war criminals. Some Cambodians, however, are not sure they want war crime trials. They say that the trials will only bring up hatred again and may even destroy the peace that has taken so long to come to Cambodia. Also, some Khmer Rouge leaders, including Pol Pot, are dead or already pardoned. Other Cambodians say that the trials will finally bring justice to the people of Cambodia, who suffered so terribly during the Pol Pot era.

Immigration

Most of the first generation of Cambodians who now call the United States or Canada home arrived as refugees after the Khmer Rouge era. Few Cambodians lived outside their country before the 1980s, but their terrible lives under the Khmer Rouge made them flee the starvation and destruction. Most of these immigrants first stayed in refugee camps along the border between Thailand and Cambodia before being accepted into another country. Some immigrants spent as many as five to ten years in the camps, and many children were born in or grew up in the camps.

Cambodians fleeing war in the 1980s were accepted by a number of countries: 150,000 refugees resettled in the United States and a total of 70,000 settled in France, Australia, Canada, and Spain. There are now Khmer communities scattered throughout the United States and Canada. In Canada, Cambodians live in Montreal, Toronto, and many other cities.

The journey from the bombed rice fields of Cambodia into the busy, crowded cities of North America has not been an easy one for many Cambodian immigrants. Most of them, however, have worked hard to cope with the new opportunities immigration has given them and to renew their lives after decades of war.

Below: **Refugee camps along the Thai border housed thousands of Cambodians after the horrific Pol Pot era.**

Cambodians in North America

Cambodian refugees saw the United States as *thanh sour* (than soo-uh), or paradise. Nearly all of them arrived in a desperate state, with no money or possessions. Many had lost family members and were undernourished and exhausted by twenty years of war, hunger, and fear. A large proportion were suffering from physical or mental illnesses because of their horrendous experiences under the Khmer Rouge and in the refugee camps. Searching for surviving relatives scattered around the world has been an important task for Cambodian families. Some Cambodians travel a long way to attend family reunions.

Fifteen years after the first wave of immigrants, there are Buddhist temples and monks and many Khmer cultural networks and associations in Canada and the United States. Cambodian children go to school with American children, and are growing up as North Americans. Their culture is already different from that of their parents. Among these Cambodian-Americans, a lot of interest exists in learning about the country many have never known or knew only during war. Organizations set up to preserve Khmer culture among Cambodian-Americans include the Khmer Studies Institute and the Cambodian-American Heritage, Inc. (CAHI).

Left: **A Cambodian man in Long Beach, California, reads an article on Pol Pot's death in a Khmer-language newspaper in April 1998. Long Beach has the largest population of Cambodians in the United States.**

Cambodian Women in North America

More than half the Cambodian immigrants to North America were women or families headed by a woman. This is because men were more often the victims of the Khmer Rouge.

Women have had to bear much of the burden of settling into totally different countries and lifestyles, as well as having to endure the loss of many of their family members, husbands, or children. Cambodian women immigrants had additional problems in trying to adapt to the new culture. Most of them were not used to running water, electricity, living in apartments, and harsh, cold winters. Many could not read or write. Those who had been educated or were wealthy had been the targets of the Khmer Rouge and suffered tremendously.

Cambodian women in the United States also had to assume new societal and gender roles. In a traditional Cambodian household, the man was the breadwinner, and the woman looked after the children and the house. Many Cambodian women who arrived in America had lost their husbands in the war and had to assume the roles of breadwinners. Younger Cambodian women have also started pursuing higher education in political science, humanities, and law.

Above: **Today, the descendants of Cambodian immigrants have assimilated into mainstream American culture. Many young Cambodian-Americans are pursuing higher education in top American universities.**

Left: **The first edition of the English language *Phnom Penh Post* was launched in July 1992. American publisher Michael Hayes headed the team that brought the independent newspaper to the country, the first of its kind in two decades.**

North Americans in Cambodia

Small communities of North Americans work and live in Phnom Penh and other Cambodian towns. Most are temporary residents, however, and they live in Cambodia for a period of time while they work on governmental or non-governmental projects. Some represent their countries as diplomatic officials, military staff, volunteers, or teachers. Other North Americans in Cambodia include business people, historians, artists, political scientists, and others who come to study some aspect of Cambodian culture.

Cultural Exchanges

Americans and Cambodians in North America are making important contributions to the revival of Cambodian culture. Scholars in North America have been working to preserve or rescue Cambodian art or make it more widely known. For example, Cornell University in the United States has begun a project to microfilm old documents in Khmer script because so many were burned or lost during the Khmer Rouge era.

In 1998, the National Museum of Arts in Phnom Penh sent some of Cambodia's finest works of art on a traveling exhibition to Washington, D.C.

The Killing Fields

The most famous Cambodian immigrants are Dith Pran and Haing S. Ngor. Photojournalist Dith Pran and American reporter Sydney Schanberg covered the Cambodian civil war in the 1970s. When the Khmer Rouge took over, Pran, Schanberg, and two foreign journalists were arrested and awaited execution. Pran saved the foreign reporters' lives when he persuaded the soldiers that they were French. The four then found refuge in the French embassy in Phnom Penh. The journalists were soon forced to leave Cambodia, and Dith Pran was sent to the countryside where he disguised his identity. He lived through four years of torture and starvation. The story of Pran's life and his reunion with Schanberg is retold in the 1984 movie, *The Killing Fields*. Pran now lives in the United States and has worked for the *New York Times*, the United Nations High Commission for Refugees, and the Red Cross, as well as on many projects to tell the world about the tragedy in Cambodia.

The Killing Fields has won many awards and is a powerful reminder of the atrocities in Cambodia during the Pol Pot era. Cambodian doctor Haing S. Ngor, who had never acted before, won an Academy Award for his portrayal of Pran in the movie. Ngor was himself tortured and lost almost every member of his family during the Pol Pot era. Ngor has devoted much of his time and money to helping refugees from his country. In 1996, Ngor was shot to death by robbers in Los Angeles.

Left: **In March 1985, Dith Pran (*right*) and Haing S. Ngor (*left*) attended the annual British Academy of Film and Television Arts (BAFTA) awards ceremony in London.**

Above: Many treasures from Angkor are housed in the National Museum in Phnom Penh.

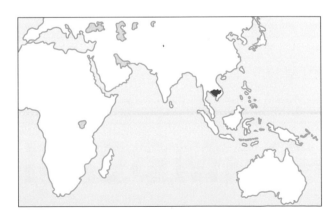

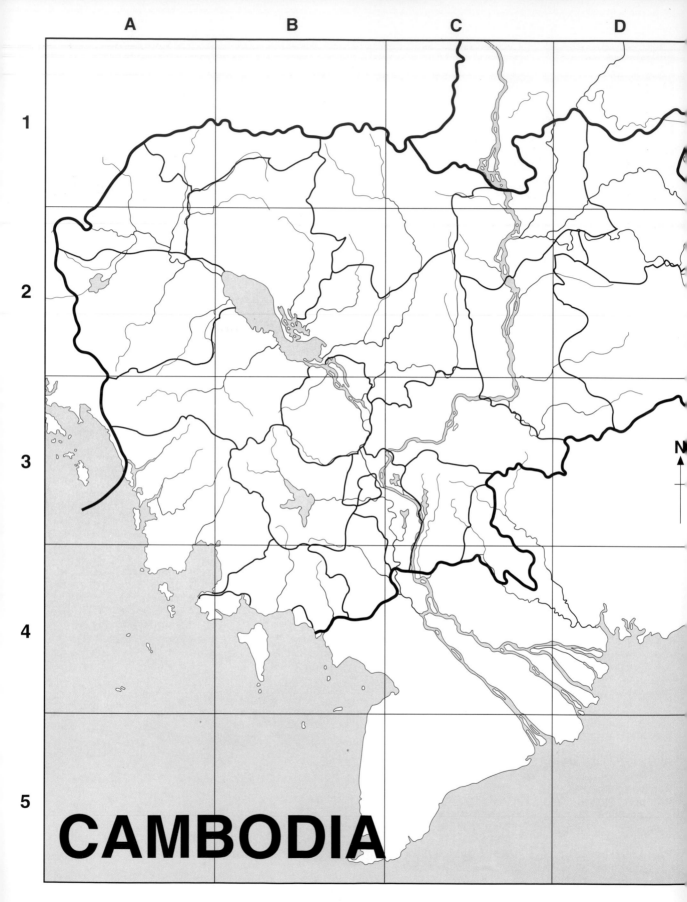

CAMBODIA

How Is Your Geography?

Learning to identify the main geographical areas and points of a country can be challenging. Although it may seem difficult at first to memorize the locations and spellings of major cities or the names of mountain ranges, rivers, deserts, lakes, and other prominent physical features, the end result of this effort can be very rewarding. Places you previously did not know existed will suddenly come to life when referred to in world news, whether in newspapers, television reports, or other books and reference sources. This knowledge will make you feel a bit closer to the rest of the world, with its fascinating variety of cultures and physical geography.

Used in a classroom setting, the instructor can make duplicates of this map using a copy machine. (PLEASE DO NOT WRITE IN THIS BOOK!) Students can then fill in any requested information on their individual map copies. Used one-on-one, the student can also make copies of the map on a copy machine and use them as a study tool. The student can practice identifying place names and geographical features on his or her own.

Below: **Rows of Buddha statues lead the way to the main temple at the ancient city of Angkor Thom.**

Cambodia at a Glance

Official Name	Kingdom of Cambodia (Preahreacheanachakr Kampuchea)
Capital	Phnom Penh
Official Language	Khmer
Population	12,212,306 (July 2000 estimate)
Land Area	70,238 square miles (181,916 square kilometers)
Provinces	Banteay Mean Cheay, Batdambang, Kampong Cham, Kampong Chhnang, Kampong Spoe, Kampong Thum, Kampot, Kandal, Kaoh Kong, Krachen, Mondol Kiri, Otdar Mean Cheay, Pouthisat, Preah Vihear, Prey Veng, Rotanah Kiri, Siem Reab, Stoeng Treng, Svay Rieng, Takev
Municipalities	Keb, Phnum Penh, Preah Seihanu (Sihanoukville)
Major Cities	Batdambang, Kampong Cham, Kampong Chhnang, Phnom Penh, Pouthisat
Highest Point	Phnom Aoral 5,948 feet (1,813 meters)
Longest River	Mekong River
Largest Lake	Tonle Sap (Great Lake)
Major Ethnic Groups	Khmer (90 percent), Vietnamese (5 percent), Chinese (1 percent), Others (4 percent)
Official Religion	Theravada Buddhism
Famous Leaders	Jayavarman VII, Hun Sen, Pol Pot, Norodom Sihanouk, Suryavarman II
Main Trade Partners	Hong Kong, Indonesia, Japan, Malaysia, Singapore, Thailand, the United States
Important Festivals	Independence Day, King's Birthday, Khmer New Year, Water Festival
Currency	Cambodian riel (3,735 riels = U.S. $1 as of August 2001)

Opposite: **The Royal Palace in Phnom Penh was built by the French in 1884.**

Glossary

Khmer Vocabulary

achar (ah-char): a shaman, ritualist, or spiritual healer.

apsaras (ap-sah-rahs): heavenly dancers.

charabap (cha-rah-bap): luxurious silk, often woven with gold and silver thread. It is normally woven for important ceremonies at the royal court.

devarajas (de-vah-rah-jahs): god-kings.

krama (krah-mah): large checkered head scarf worn over the head and neck as protection from the sun.

kru (kru): spirit healer.

nagas (nah-gahs): mythical snakes.

neak ta (ne-ak tah): ancestral spirits.

pin peat (pin pe-aht): musical ensemble, which normally features quadruple reed oboes, xylophones, gongs, barrel drums, and small cymbals.

prahok (prah-hok): fish paste.

ram vong (ram vong): a popular Cambodian folk dance.

rup areak (rup ah-re-ak): spirit medium.

sampots (sahm-pots): loose-fitting garments wrapped around the waist and worn by women.

sarongs (sah-rohngs): large pieces of cloth wrapped around the waist.

singhas (sing-ngahs): guardian lions.

thmup (tee-moop): witch.

tuk trey (tak trey): fish sauce.

wat (wat): temple.

English Vocabulary

alluvial: made up of sand, clay, and other materials left behind by moving water.

amputated: cut off or removed by a surgical procedure.

amulet: an object worn on the body and believed to protect one from evil spirits or harm.

annihilation: total destruction.

aristocrats: people with high social standing, inherited wealth, and often possessing titles.

astrologer: a person who foretells a person's character and future by studying the movements of the sun, moon, stars, and planets.

autonomy: self-government.

coalition government: a government made up of members from two or more political parties.

communism: a system of government based on the common ownership of property.

Confucianists: people who follow the teachings of Chinese philosopher and teacher Confucius, who advocated loyalty, wisdom, and honesty.

contentious: marked by controversy and dispute.

coup: an unexpected political uprising.

deforestation: the large-scale cutting down or destruction of trees.

dictator: a ruler with absolute power and authority.

ecosystem: a system made up of the plant and animal community interacting with each other and with the environment.

erosion: the gradual depletion of rock or soil.

exodus: the mass departure of a large group of people.

exorcised: removed unhappy or painful memories from the mind.

genocide: the systematic killing of an entire community or ethnic group.

guerrillas: people who form an unofficial army to fight against the existing political order.

homogeneous: having similar characteristics or qualities.

icon: an image, often religious, of devotion.

intelligentsia: the class of educated people and intellectuals in a community.

irrigation: a means of supplying water to a dry area.

karma: the belief, in the Buddhist and Hindu religions, that a person's actions in this life will affect his or her future lives.

Mahayana Buddhism: a form of Buddhism that follows a liberal interpretation of the Buddha's teachings.

maim: to cripple or cause the loss of some parts of the body, such as the limbs.

monsoons: strong, seasonal winds.

municipalities: cities or towns that have their own government and governing officials for local affairs.

mythological: relating to a popular belief or tradition that has no factual basis.

nationalism: the desire for political and national independence.

naturalist: a person who studies nature.

nirvana: the highest state of spiritual enlightenment a person can achieve in the Buddhist religion.

novice: a person who is preparing to become a monk or a nun in a monastery or convent.

orthodox: adhering to the more conventional and traditional teachings of a religion or of politics.

patriarch: the male head of a group.

persecuted: brutally and unfairly treated because of reasons related to politics, race, or religion.

Pisakh Bochea: a Buddhist festival celebrating Buddha's birth, his enlightenment, and his attainment of eternal bliss.

precepts: rules that guide one in correct moral conduct and behavior.

radical: extreme; drastic.

rehabilitating: restoring to a good condition so that it can be used again.

resins: sticky substances produced by trees.

sorcery: magical power.

sumptuary laws: laws that regulate expenditure and prevent extravagance on moral and religious grounds.

syllabus: subjects in a course of study.

Taoists: people who follow the teaching of Chinese philosopher Lao Tzu, who advocated simplicity and selflessness.

Theravada Buddhists: Buddhists who follow a conservative interpretation of the Buddha's teachings. They believe that one cannot attain enlightenment while living the life of a lay person.

UNESCO: the United Nations Educational, Scientific, and Cultural Organization. Created in 1946, UNESCO promotes peace through international projects in education, science, and culture.

ziggurat: a pyramid-shaped temple tower in ancient Babylon, with terraces that become smaller as they advance up the tower.

More Books to Read

Angkat: The Cambodian Cinderella. Jewell Reinhart Coburn (Shen's Books)

Cambodia. Cultures of the World series. Sean Sheehan (Benchmark Books)

Cambodia in Pictures. Visual Geography series. (Lerner Publications Company)

Cambodia. Major World Nations series. Claudia Canesso (Chelsea House)

Children in Exile: The Story of a Cross-Cultural Family. Thekla Clark (Ecco Press)

The Clay Marble. Minfong Ho (Sunburst Books)

Dance in Cambodia. Images of Asia series. Toni Samantha Phim and Ashley Thompson (Oxford University Press)

Little Brother. Allan Baillie (Puffin)

The People of Cambodia. Dolly Brittan (Powerkids Press)

The Site of Angkor. Images of Asia series. Jacques Dumarçay (Oxford University Press)

Videos

In the Shadow of Angkor Wat. (Home Vision Cinema)

Lost Spirits of Cambodia. (A & E Home Video)

Mysteries of Asia: Jewels in the Jungle. (TLC Video)

Raising the Bamboo Curtain: Awakening Burma, Cambodia, and Vietnam. (Questar Inc.)

Web Sites

www.cambodian.com/history.htm

www.camnet.com.kh/camweb.htm

www.embassy.org/cambodia/

members.aol.com/cambodia/index.htm

www.odci.gov/cia/publications/factbook/cb.html

Due to the dynamic nature of the Internet, some web sites stay current longer than others. To find additional web sites, use a reliable search engine with one or more of the following keywords to help you locate information about Cambodia. Keywords: *Angkor Wat, Cambodia, Dith Pran, Hun Sen, Khmer Rouge, Norodom Sihanouk, Phnom Penh, Pol Pot.*

Index